INSIDE GUIDES

ANIMAL REPRODUCTION

Written by
DAVID BURNIE

DORLING KINDERSLEY
London • New York • Stuttgart • Moscow • Sydney

D1421234

Empid flies
mating

A DORLING KINDERSLEY BOOK

Editor Julie Ferris
Senior art editor Jill Plank
DTP designer Nicola Studdart
Senior managing editor Gillian Denton
Senior managing art editor Julia Harris
Picture research Kate Duncan
Production Charlotte Traill

Photography Geoff Brightling
Modelmakers Peter Minister Model FX,
Dave Morgan, Chris Reynolds and the BBC team,
and Gary and Lissi Staab

First published in Great Britain in 1998
by Dorling Kindersley Limited,
9 Henrietta Street, London WC2E 8PS
2 4 6 8 10 9 7 5 3 1

Copyright © 1998
Dorling Kindersley Limited,
London
Visit us on the
World Wide Web
at http://www.dk.com

A CIP catalogue record for this book is
available from the British Library.
ISBN 0-75135-656-5

Reproduced in Italy by
GRB Editrice S.r.l., Verona
Printed in Singapore by Toppan

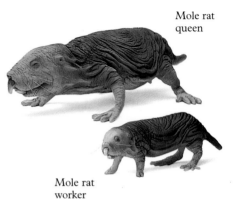

Mole rat
queen

Mole rat
worker

Cross-section
of a tapeworm
showing the
reproductive
organs

Development inside a
chicken's egg

Contents

Juvenile aphids

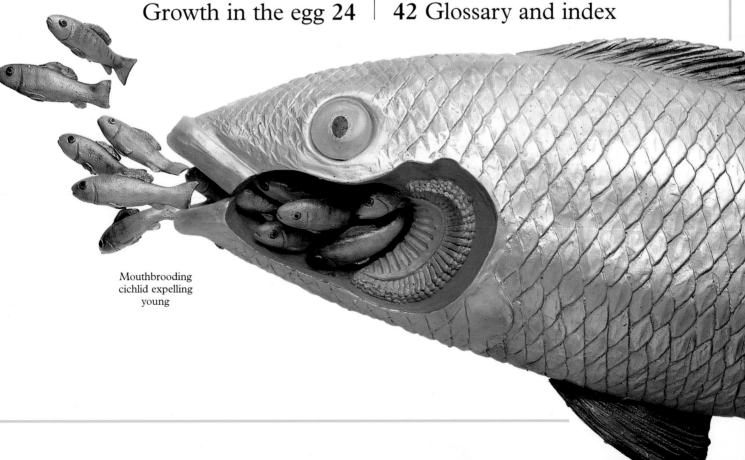

Mouthbrooding cichlid expelling young

What is reproduction?

Reproduction is the most important feature of living things. Without it, they would slowly die out, and nothing would be left to take their place. Reproduction allows different species to thrive and spread, and it allows living things to pass on their characteristics. In the animal world, reproduction works in many different ways. Some animals can reproduce entirely on their own, while others need a partner of the opposite sex, or one that is both sexes at once. Many animals lay eggs, others give birth to live young, and some animals, such as the sea anemone, simply split in half. The tiniest animals can produce hundreds of offspring in the space of a few weeks, but the largest – such as elephants and whales – often take years to raise a single baby.

In at the finish
Only about one per cent of sperm come within striking distance of the egg cell.

Feathers dry out soon after hatching

Jacket of jelly
A jelly-like layer called the zona pellucida surrounds the egg cell.

Into the outside world
As this baby ostrich pecks its way out of its egg, it looks as though it is just starting life. But like most other animals, its life actually begins at the moment of fertilization, when a sperm and egg cell join together.

Delivering genes
The head of a sperm cell contains a set of the father's genes.

Awesome odds
Over 500 million sperm cells may make their way towards the egg cell, but only one will fertilize it.

Young hydra budding from parent

Population explosion
In the course of their short lives, female blowflies can lay over 600 eggs. Animals that breed quickly have many predators that keep their numbers in check, so there is no possibility of flies overrunning the Earth.

Lone parent
Some animals, such as this hydra, can reproduce without having to find a mate. A hydra grows buds that turn into new animals. Other lone parents can produce young from eggs that develop without being fertilized.

On the move
Sperm cells swim towards the egg cell by wriggling their tails.

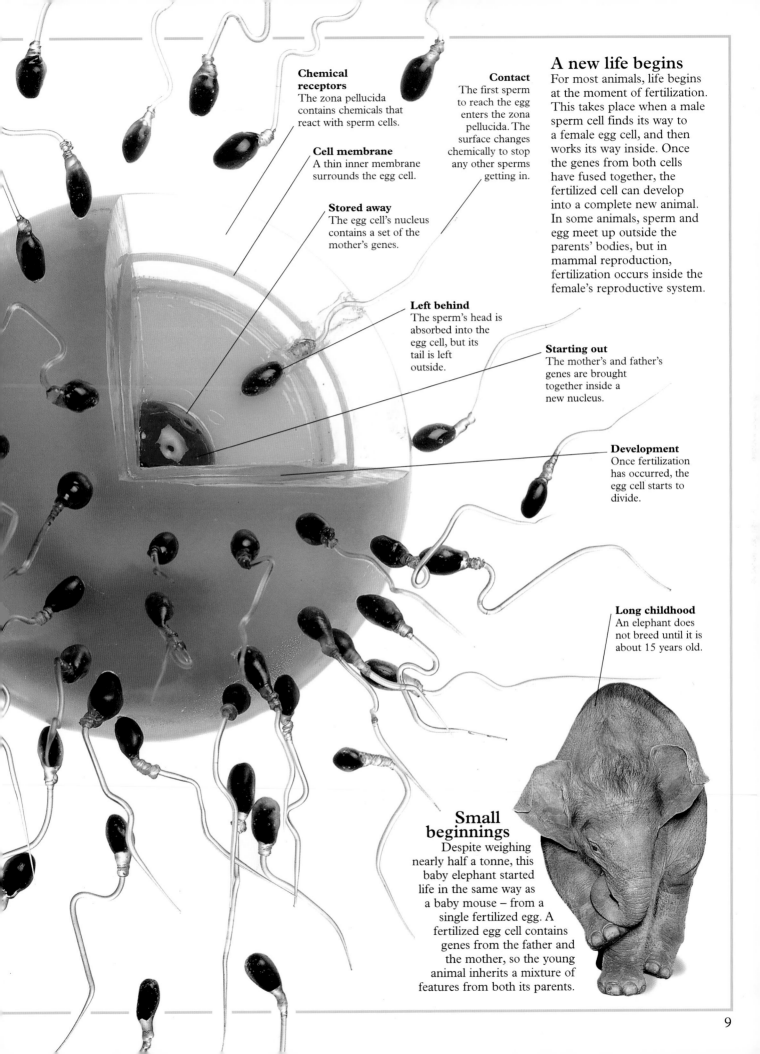

Chemical receptors
The zona pellucida contains chemicals that react with sperm cells.

Cell membrane
A thin inner membrane surrounds the egg cell.

Stored away
The egg cell's nucleus contains a set of the mother's genes.

Contact
The first sperm to reach the egg enters the zona pellucida. The surface changes chemically to stop any other sperms getting in.

Left behind
The sperm's head is absorbed into the egg cell, but its tail is left outside.

Starting out
The mother's and father's genes are brought together inside a new nucleus.

Development
Once fertilization has occurred, the egg cell starts to divide.

A new life begins

For most animals, life begins at the moment of fertilization. This takes place when a male sperm cell finds its way to a female egg cell, and then works its way inside. Once the genes from both cells have fused together, the fertilized cell can develop into a complete new animal. In some animals, sperm and egg meet up outside the parents' bodies, but in mammal reproduction, fertilization occurs inside the female's reproductive system.

Long childhood
An elephant does not breed until it is about 15 years old.

Small beginnings

Despite weighing nearly half a tonne, this baby elephant started life in the same way as a baby mouse – from a single fertilized egg. A fertilized egg cell contains genes from the father and the mother, so the young animal inherits a mixture of features from both its parents.

Single parents

Microscopic protozoan dividing in two

For small freshwater animals called hydras, reproduction is a simple matter. An adult hydra grows small "buds" on the side of its body, and each of these slowly turns into a complete new animal. "Budding" is an example of asexual reproduction – a way of making young that involves just one parent. This kind of reproduction can be quick and easy, but it does have one important disadvantage: unlike sexual reproduction it always produces young identical to the parent, and any weak points the parent had are duplicated in the young. Hydras have a way around this problem. Like aphids (pp. 30–31), they normally use asexual reproduction when there is plenty of food and conditions for survival are good, but switch to sexual reproduction when times become harder.

Collecting a meal
The hydra uses its ring of tentacles to pull food towards its mouth.

Hollow insides
A hydra's body is like a hollow tube. It is open at the mouth, but usually sealed at the base.

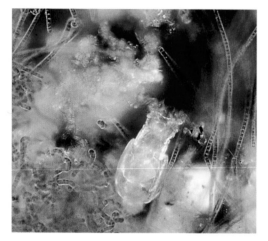

Rotifers
Microscopic rotifers are among the world's smallest animals. They live in water and damp places, and most of them are less than 0.5 mm (0.02 in) long. One of the reasons for their success is that the females can reproduce rapidly without having to mate. In many species, males have never been found.

Digesting food
Cells lining the digestive cavity produce chemicals that break down the hydra's food.

Hydras are about 5 mm (0.2 in) long

Attached
Hydras attach their base to underwater plants.

Living scales
Like their relatives aphids (pp. 30–31), scale insects often reproduce without having to mate. Their eggs develop into young without being fertilized. Female scale insects live by sucking sap from plants, and hardly look like insects at all. They spend their adult lives fastened to plants and are protected by a hard scale-like shield. Male scale insects are much smaller. Unlike the females, they have wings and are able to fly.

Paralyzed prey
This young water flea has been immobilized by stinging cells on the hydra's tentacles.

Deadly stings
Each tentacle is armed with dozens of stinging cells, or nematocysts.

Changing shape
A hydra can pull in its tentacles, or spread them wide to catch food.

Second option
When hydras reproduce sexually, they make both egg and sperm cells. This bump is an ovary – an organ that will produce a single egg.

Tentacular ring
Hydras usually have five or six tentacles, arranged in a ring around their mouths.

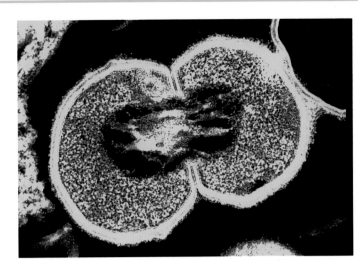

Dividing bacterium
This bacterium, a microscopic organism, is about to divide in two, producing two new cells. In good conditions, bacteria can divide every 20 minutes, which means that a single bacterium can quickly produce many millions of offspring. This kind of rapid reproduction makes some bacteria quite dangerous because they can rapidly spread through food or the body.

No escape
This tiny worm is being drawn inside the hydra's body, where it will be digested.

Budding baby
Although they are still fastened together, this parent hydra and its young are two separate animals. At first, the young hydra shares food that its parent has caught, because its digestive cavity is connected to its parent's. However, as its tentacles develop, it starts to catch food for itself. The young hydra has just seized a meal, and it will soon be ready to take up life on its own.

Moving along
Hydras can move by taking steps with their tentacles. In emergencies, they can escape from danger in a series of slow-motion somersaults.

Slow separation
Flatworms, or planarians, sometimes reproduce asexually simply by leaving part of themselves behind. The flatworm's body starts to narrow, and the rear part eventually pulls itself away. The rear grows a new head, while the front of the worm grows a new tail. These two flatworms have narrowed bodies, and they will soon divide in this way.

Ready for action
A hydra's tentacles are sensitive to touch, and also to chemicals produced by passing animals.

Torn in two
Sea anemones are close relatives of hydras. Although most produce young by sexual reproduction, some can also reproduce asexually by tearing themselves in two. This sea anemone is part way through the process.

Courting couples

Male stickleback fish displaying bright red courting colours

In the animal world, it is usually the male's job to attract a partner. Males do this by using special courtship displays. These displays show that the male is strong and healthy, and that he belongs to the right species. If a female is sufficiently impressed by a male's courtship display, she will allow him to approach her and mate. Courtship displays vary enormously between different animals. Some attract attention through noises, while others show off eyecatching body parts.

Changing colour
The claw often becomes brightly coloured in the breeding season.

This fiddler crab's claw is outstretched at the start.

The male then raises its giant claw as high as it can.

The claw quickly drops back to rest in front of the crab.

The fiddler crab rests for a while before the display begins again.

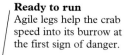

All puffed up
Male frigate birds attract females with the help of an inflatable throat pouch that looks like a red balloon. During the breeding season each male looks for a suitable nest site, and puffs up his pouch to attract females as they fly overhead.

Ready to run
Agile legs help the crab speed into its burrow at the first sign of danger.

Signals on the shore
Fiddler crabs live in the mud of mangrove swamps. At low tide, they come out of their burrows, and the males signal to females by waving a single giant claw. Each kind of fiddler crab uses a different sequence of movements, so females are always attracted to the right species of mate. Although fiddler crabs are tiny, the male's display is easy to see across the flat mud.

Pulling power
Males with the biggest claws attract the most females.

Either side
The giant claw can be either on the left or the right.

Clumsy claw
The crab's claw is too big to be used for feeding. It is only used for signalling.

Animal attraction
Some male birds, like this ruff, gather together during the breeding season, and display in special courtship arenas called leks. Females watch as the males perform the displays, and then mate with whichever one impresses them the most.

Weight lifters
Extra-large muscles raise the claw, and open and close the pincers. The crab often rests the heavy claw in the mud.

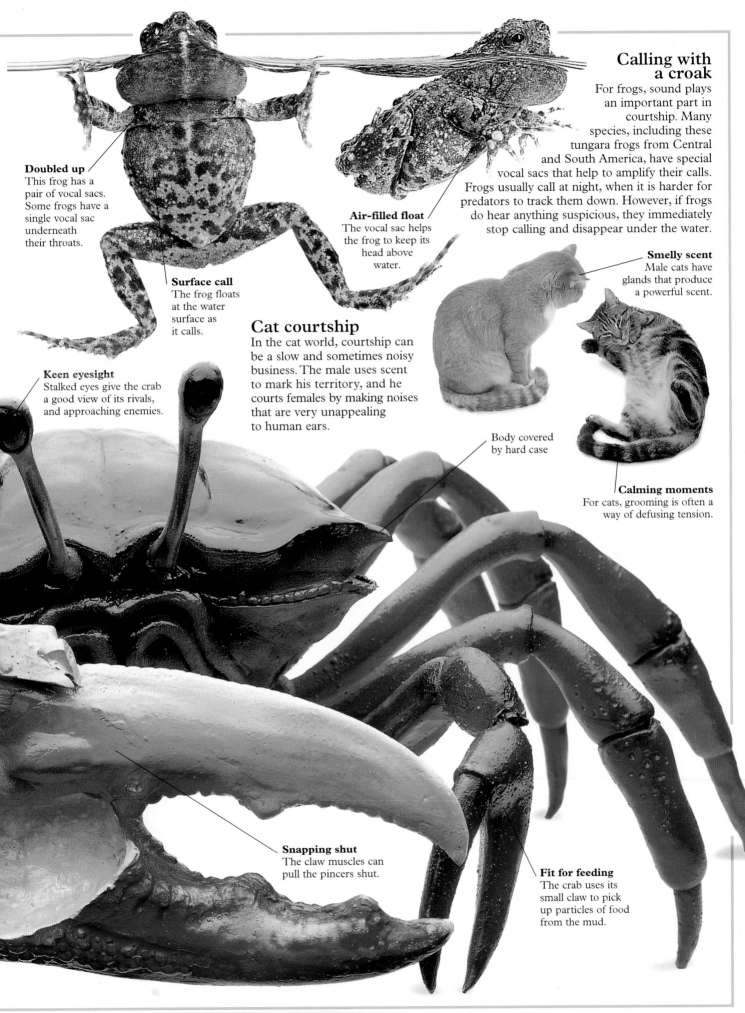

Doubled up
This frog has a pair of vocal sacs. Some frogs have a single vocal sac underneath their throats.

Surface call
The frog floats at the water surface as it calls.

Air-filled float
The vocal sac helps the frog to keep its head above water.

Calling with a croak

For frogs, sound plays an important part in courtship. Many species, including these tungara frogs from Central and South America, have special vocal sacs that help to amplify their calls. Frogs usually call at night, when it is harder for predators to track them down. However, if frogs do hear anything suspicious, they immediately stop calling and disappear under the water.

Smelly scent
Male cats have glands that produce a powerful scent.

Cat courtship

In the cat world, courtship can be a slow and sometimes noisy business. The male uses scent to mark his territory, and he courts females by making noises that are very unappealing to human ears.

Body covered by hard case

Calming moments
For cats, grooming is often a way of defusing tension.

Keen eyesight
Stalked eyes give the crab a good view of its rivals, and approaching enemies.

Snapping shut
The claw muscles can pull the pincers shut.

Fit for feeding
The crab uses its small claw to pick up particles of food from the mud.

All in one

When adult slugs or snails get together to breed, they do not have to worry about finding a partner of the opposite sex. This is because most slugs and snails are both male and female at once, which means that any two adults can mate. After a long and slimy courtship, each animal fertilizes its partner, and both partners then slither away to lay a batch of eggs. Animals that are both male and female are called hermaphrodites. They include a wide variety of invertebrates (animals without backbones), but only a few vertebrates. As well as true hermaphrodites, the animal world also includes species that mix up the sexes in a different way. These animals start adult life as one sex, and then slowly change into the other.

Love dart
Snail courtship really gets moving when one of the snails fires a "love dart" into its partner. The love dart is made of a chalky substance, and it is sharp enough to penetrate its partner's skin. This dart has fallen to the ground.

Hermaphrodite fish
Many fish change sex as they get older, but the brightly striped comber is one of the few species that is a true hermaphrodite. Unlike a slug or snail, the comber can fertilize its own eggs, which means that it does not have to find a partner in order to breed.

Give and take
When snails mate, each one unfolds its penis and inserts it into its partner. The two snails remain locked together for up to six hours, while they each deliver and receive a package of sperm called a spermatophore. After mating, these slowly break open, and the sperms fertilize each snail's eggs.

Joining the pile
Slipper limpets fasten themselves to each other's shells, and live in piles of up to nine animals. The oldest limpets, at the bottom of the pile, are always female. All limpets start out as male, but gradually turn into females when more limpets join the pile.

Hanging by a thread

When great grey slugs are ready to mate, they climb up a wall or a tree, and then lower themselves into mid-air on a thread of slime. Once upside down, they lower their penises, which unfold into a shape like an umbrella. After mating, the two slugs crawl back up the thread, eating it as they go.

Penises twined together

Ovotestis produces both eggs and sperms

Laying eggs

Garden snails lay their eggs in early summer, when the ground is warm but damp. Each snail digs a shallow pit in some loose earth, and then drops about 50 pearly eggs into the hole. The eggs hatch into miniature snails with almost transparent shells, which crawl up to the surface.

Mucus glands
These glands produce slime that is used when the snails mate.

Sperm storage
A sperm package is stored in this chamber after it is received from the other snail. The package's wrapping dissolves after several days.

Dart sac
This muscular chamber contains the snail's dart, which is fired at the start of courtship.

Flagellum
This whip-like tube makes the substances that form the wrapping of the sperm package.

Retractor muscle

Penis
When mating is over, the snail's penis is pulled back into its body by a special retractor muscle.

Muscular foot

Reproductive duct
This carries sperms from an organ called the ovotestis, and also stores the eggs.

Albumen gland
This forms a jelly-like substance that coats the snail's eggs. It helps to stop them drying out.

Close encounters

For an animal to breed sexually, sperm cells must meet up with egg cells, so the egg cells can be fertilized. In water, most animals use external fertilization. They simply release their eggs and sperm into the water around them, and fertilization takes place when the male and female cells meet. But on land, this kind of fertilization is quite rare, because eggs and sperm quickly dry out. Instead, most land animals use a different method, called internal fertilization. The male and female pair up and mate, and the male inserts his sperm into his partner.

External fertilization
During the breeding season, male toads pair up with females. The male grips his partner using his strong front legs, and is almost impossible to dislodge. When the two toads reach a pond, the female starts to lay her long string of eggs. As soon as the eggs begin to emerge, the male releases his sperm into the water, which ensures that the eggs are fertilized.

Eggs aboard
At the beginning of the breeding season, a female toad's body is swollen with several thousand eggs.

Tight hold
The male toad grips his partner with his front legs. To stop him from slipping off, he has special roughened pads on his thumbs.

Hanging on
During mating, empid flies hang from a twig. The male grips the twig with his front legs, and uses his other four legs to grip his partner.

Shaping silk
The male uses the flat pads on his front legs to make the silken cocoon.

Fatal encounter
This female praying mantis is finishing off an unusual meal – her male partner. Female praying mantises are larger than the males. During mating, they sometimes eat their mates, starting with the head and working downwards. Males often manage to avoid this gruesome fate, but if a male does lose his head, the rest of his body completes the mating process.

Mating cats
The time that mating takes varies between one kind of animal and another. In some butterflies, mating can take several hours. In cats, it is over in a matter of minutes.

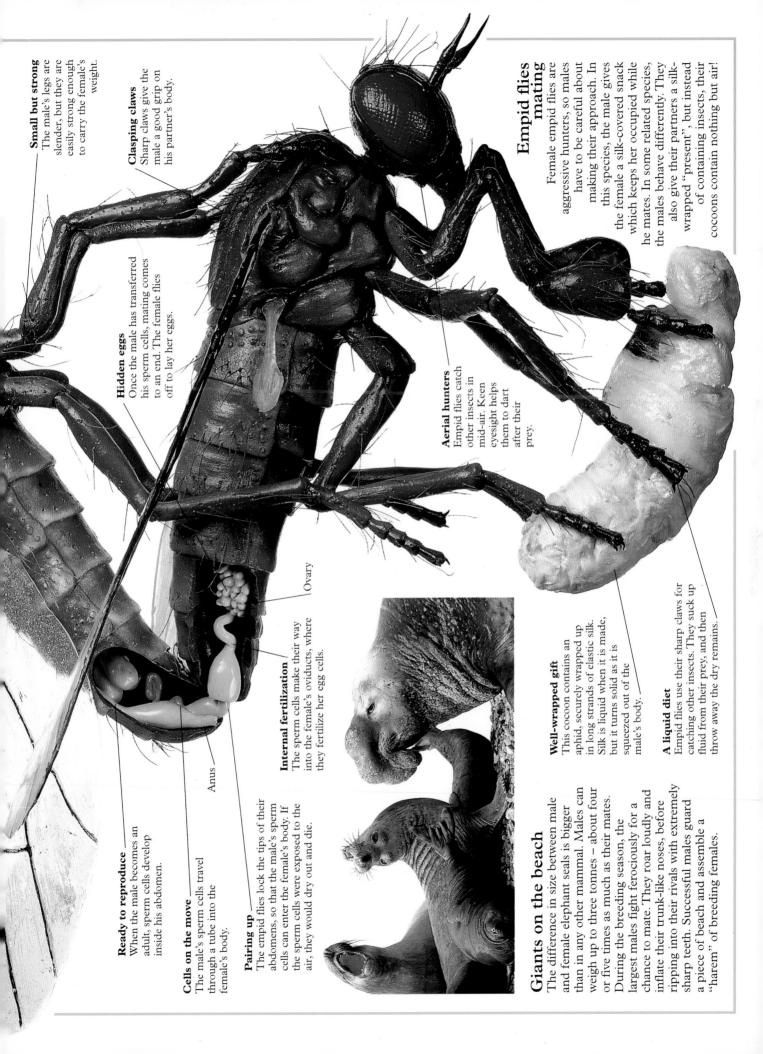

Small but strong
The male's legs are slender, but they are easily strong enough to carry the female's weight.

Clasping claws
Sharp claws give the male a good grip on his partner's body.

Hidden eggs
Once the male has transferred his sperm cells, mating comes to an end. The female flies off to lay her eggs.

Ready to reproduce
When the male becomes an adult, sperm cells develop inside his abdomen.

Cells on the move
The male's sperm cells travel through a tube into the female's body.

Pairing up
The empid flies lock the tips of their abdomens, so that the male's sperm cells can enter the female's body. If the sperm cells were exposed to the air, they would dry out and die.

Anus

Ovary

Internal fertilization
The sperm cells make their way into the female's oviducts, where they fertilize her egg cells.

Aerial hunters
Empid flies catch other insects in mid-air. Keen eyesight helps them to dart after their prey.

Empid flies mating

Female empid flies are aggressive hunters, so males have to be careful about making their approach. In this species, the male gives the female a silk-covered snack which keeps her occupied while he mates. In some related species, the males behave differently. They also give their partners a silk-wrapped "present", but instead of containing insects, their cocoons contain nothing but air!

Well-wrapped gift
This cocoon contains an aphid, securely wrapped up in long strands of elastic silk. Silk is liquid when it is made, but it turns solid as it is squeezed out of the male's body.

A liquid diet
Empid flies use their sharp claws for catching other insects. They suck up fluid from their prey, and then throw away the dry remains.

Giants on the beach

The difference in size between male and female elephant seals is bigger than in any other mammal. Males can weigh up to three tonnes – about four or five times as much as their mates. During the breeding season, the largest males fight ferociously for a chance to mate. They roar loudly and inflate their trunk-like noses, before ripping into their rivals with extremely sharp teeth. Successful males guard a piece of beach and assemble a "harem" of breeding females.

Extended families

The dry, dusty soil of East Africa is home to one of the world's strangest mammals – a wrinkly rodent called the naked mole rat. Mole rats not only look odd, they also breed in a very unusual way. Instead of pairing up to raise their young, they live in large family groups called colonies, and share out the work involved in staying alive. In each colony, only one female, called the queen, produces young. The other members of the colony are called workers. They forage for food, and look after the queen's offspring. Animals that live like this are called "eusocial" species.

Queen and workers
A queen naked mole rat is about 10 cm (4 in) long. She weighs about one and a half times as much as the workers, and usually has one or two male partners. Workers can be either male or female.

The royal chamber
Mole rats feed on plant roots, and live entirely underground in a network of burrows. At the heart of this network is a football-sized chamber where the queen mole rat gives birth to her young. She can have up to 12 pups in a litter, and they take a year to become adult. Chemicals in the queen's urine stop the other mole rats from having young.

Royal chamber

Nurseries

Ground level

Termite mound
Giant family groups are common in the world of insects. Termites live in groups that can be over a million strong. In proportion to their size, they build the biggest homes of all land animals. Each nest contains a single queen who, trapped in a special cell, lays up to 30,000 eggs a day.

Tight fit
Although the queen weighs more than the workers, she is still slender enough to fit through the colony's narrow tunnels.

Living excavators
Workers use their feet to shovel soil backwards when they dig.

Paper nests
Some wasps breed on their own, but many live in family groups. This wasp nest is built out of a kind of paper made of chewed-up wood fibres. It was started by a queen wasp, and then expanded by her offspring. Wasps breed very quickly in summer, but in many species, only the queens survive the winter.

Insulation
Overlapping layers of paper keep the inside of the nest warm.

Nursery area
Wasp grubs grow up in cells inside the nest.

Dental chisels
Mole rats use their front teeth to dig, and also to gnaw into their food. These teeth grow nonstop, which means they never wear down.

Trip to the toilet
Workers take the baby mole rats to the toilet burrow where they leave their droppings.

In touch
Naked mole rats do not have fur, but they do have extremely sensitive whiskers. Mole rats can also feel vibrations made by animals moving about above.

Food supply
For their first few weeks, baby mole rats feed on the queen's milk. Later, workers bring them food.

Underground eyes
Mole rats can open their eyes, but because they live underground, they hardly ever need to use them.

Eggs on board

Californian mountain kingsnakes entwined during mating

Most animals start life as a large single cell, or egg. In viviparous animals, the eggs develop inside the mother, and the young are born alive. In oviparous animals, the eggs are laid at an earlier stage, and they complete their development outside the mother's body. Nearly all the world's mammals give birth to live young, while every single species of bird lays eggs. But in the world of reptiles, things are more complicated. Some reptiles bear live young. Others, such as the Burmese python, lay eggs that take several weeks to hatch. A few species of snakes and lizards reproduce in a different way. They are ovo-viviparous, meaning that they keep their eggs in their bodies until they are ready to hatch.

Burmese python
This giant snake from southeast Asia lays up to 60 leathery-shelled eggs each time it breeds. The eggs take about 14 weeks to develop inside the mother's body, and once they are laid they take a further eight weeks to hatch. During this time the mother wraps her body around the eggs, hiding them and keeping them warm.

Stretched out
The snake's internal organs are long and slender to fit in an elongated body.

Live birth
This European common lizard is giving birth to a family of live young. Live birth is common in snakes and lizards that live in cool parts of the world, where eggs would have difficulty developing. Thanks to this method of reproduction, the common lizard manages to survive and breed north of the Arctic Circle – a remarkable feat for a cold-blooded reptile.

Cryptic pattern
Disruptive markings help to break up the snake's outline.

Secret serpent
Superb camouflage conceals the python while it hunts for prey in the shadows of the forest floor.

Snakes are legless reptiles

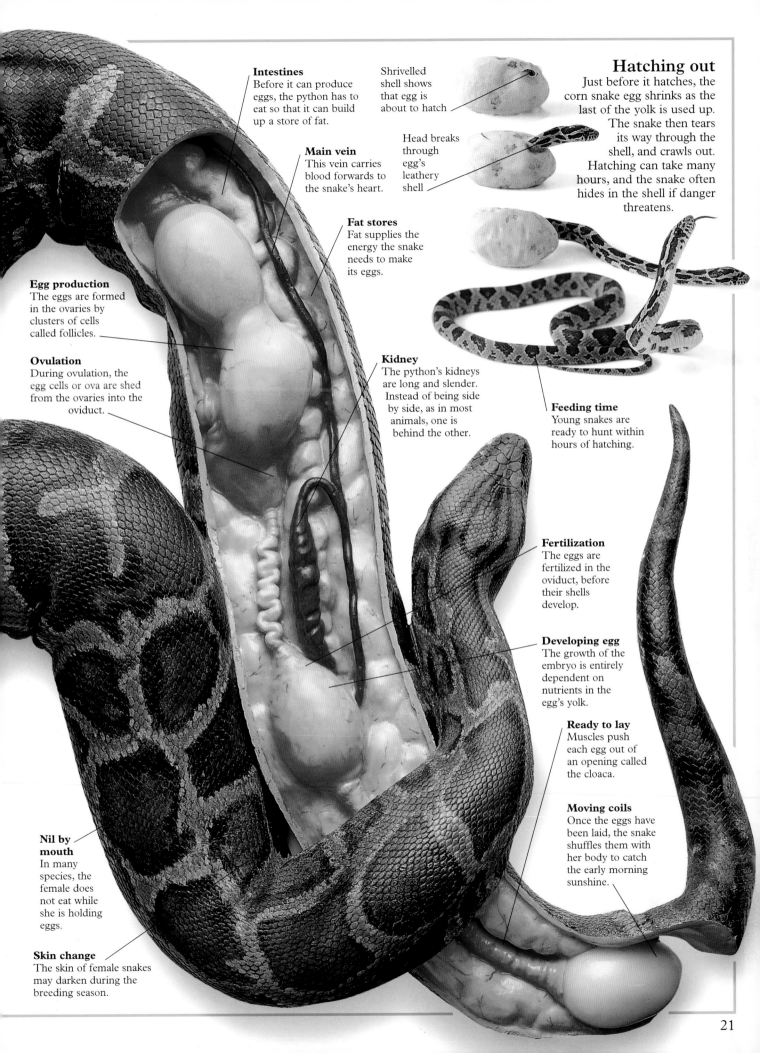

Intestines
Before it can produce eggs, the python has to eat so that it can build up a store of fat.

Shrivelled shell shows that egg is about to hatch

Main vein
This vein carries blood forwards to the snake's heart.

Head breaks through egg's leathery shell

Fat stores
Fat supplies the energy the snake needs to make its eggs.

Hatching out
Just before it hatches, the corn snake egg shrinks as the last of the yolk is used up. The snake then tears its way through the shell, and crawls out. Hatching can take many hours, and the snake often hides in the shell if danger threatens.

Egg production
The eggs are formed in the ovaries by clusters of cells called follicles.

Ovulation
During ovulation, the egg cells or ova are shed from the ovaries into the oviduct.

Kidney
The python's kidneys are long and slender. Instead of being side by side, as in most animals, one is behind the other.

Feeding time
Young snakes are ready to hunt within hours of hatching.

Fertilization
The eggs are fertilized in the oviduct, before their shells develop.

Developing egg
The growth of the embryo is entirely dependent on nutrients in the egg's yolk.

Ready to lay
Muscles push each egg out of an opening called the cloaca.

Moving coils
Once the eggs have been laid, the snake shuffles them with her body to catch the early morning sunshine.

Nil by mouth
In many species, the female does not eat while she is holding eggs.

Skin change
The skin of female snakes may darken during the breeding season.

Laying eggs

On warm summer nights, female grasshoppers search for a patch of sandy ground. They carefully dig into it with their abdomens and slowly lay batches of eggs. Like grasshoppers, many other animals take care when laying their eggs. Some bury them in the ground or fasten them to a plant, while others lay them in specially constructed nests. Nest-makers often look after their eggs until they hatch. However, other egg-layers abandon the eggs once they have been laid.

Eggs on the beach
Under the cover of darkness, ocean-going turtles crawl onto sandy beaches to lay their eggs. They use their back flippers to excavate a hole, and then slowly drop their eggs into it.

Eggs underground
Many species of grasshopper bury their eggs in the ground. This keeps the eggs moist, and protects them from hungry animals. During egg-laying, the female grasshopper's abdomen can stretch up to three times its normal length and tunnel into the ground.

Sealed in
Once the eggs have been laid, the female closes up the hole, and often seals it with quick-drying foam.

Elastic abdomen
The abdomen is covered by hard plates that are connected by softer skin. This skin stretches when the female digs downwards.

Digging down
Small flaps at the end of the abdomen open and close as she digs, forcing a hole through the ground.

Egg production
Eggs form in two rows of ovaries inside the grasshopper's abdomen.

Oviduct

Anus

Multiple batches
Some grasshoppers lay only a few eggs, but others lay up to 50 in a batch.

Filled with froth
Grasshoppers and locusts often produce froth when they lay their eggs. The froth helps keep the eggs moist.

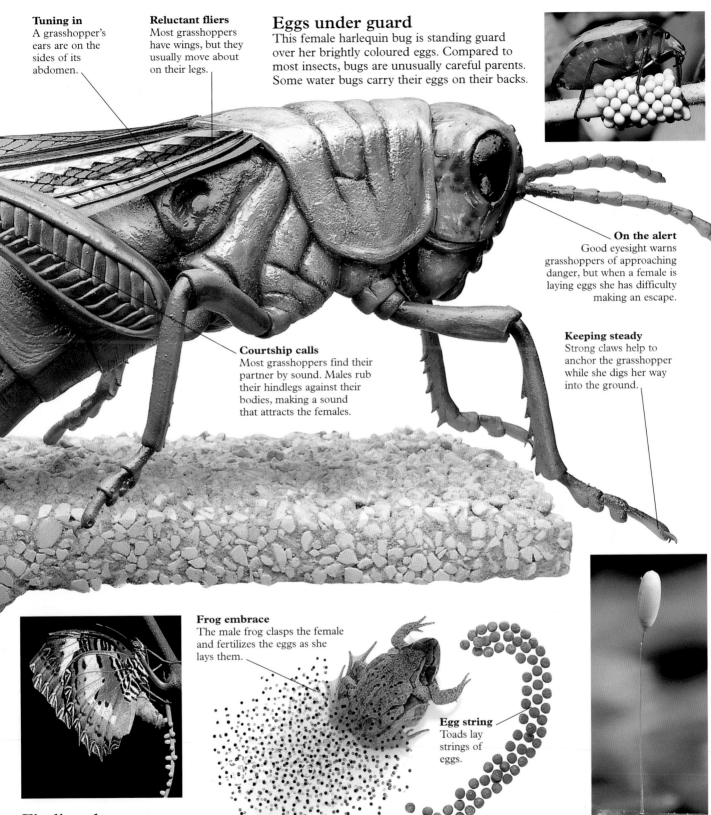

Tuning in
A grasshopper's ears are on the sides of its abdomen.

Reluctant fliers
Most grasshoppers have wings, but they usually move about on their legs.

Eggs under guard
This female harlequin bug is standing guard over her brightly coloured eggs. Compared to most insects, bugs are unusually careful parents. Some water bugs carry their eggs on their backs.

On the alert
Good eyesight warns grasshoppers of approaching danger, but when a female is laying eggs she has difficulty making an escape.

Keeping steady
Strong claws help to anchor the grasshopper while she digs her way into the ground.

Courtship calls
Most grasshoppers find their partner by sound. Males rub their hindlegs against their bodies, making a sound that attracts the females.

Frog embrace
The male frog clasps the female and fertilizes the eggs as she lays them.

Egg string
Toads lay strings of eggs.

Finding the spot
Some butterflies and moths drop their eggs from the air, but most – such as this Malay lacewing butterfly – carefully search out suitable foodplants, and then cement their eggs in position. When the caterpillars emerge from the eggs, they will have plenty of food to eat.

Laying underwater
Both frogs and toads lay eggs underwater. A female common toad can lay up to 4,000 eggs. She lays them in long strings, which she wraps around underwater plants. As soon as the eggs leave her body, the male fertilizes them. Frogs can lay as many as 20,000 eggs in one clump.

Eggs on stalks
Insect eggs make an easy meal for small animals, and many get eaten before they have a chance to hatch. Lacewings get around this problem by laying their eggs on stalks. The stalks make it harder for predators to reach.

Growth in the egg

After it has been fertilized, an egg begins to develop. Its original cell divides into two, and the new cells then divide again. Many more divisions quickly follow, as the new cells begin to rearrange themselves and develop in different ways. Bit by bit, a young animal, or embryo, starts to take shape. In a frog's egg, these remarkable changes can be seen from outside, because the jelly around the egg is transparent. In a bird's egg, an embryo develops into a fully feathered chick, hidden away by the shell.

Popping out
Young birds break their way out of their eggs, but lice, such as this head louse, have a different way of hatching. They push against the top end of the egg case, or nit, opening a special lid that lets them out. Many other insects hatch by eating their way through their shells.

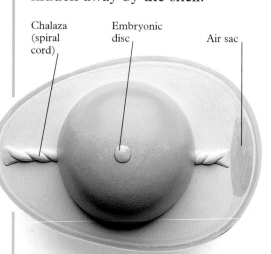

Chalaza (spiral cord) Embryonic disc Air sac

Day one
By the time the egg is laid, it already contains several thousand cells. They form a small patch called an embryonic disc, which lies on the surface of the yolk.

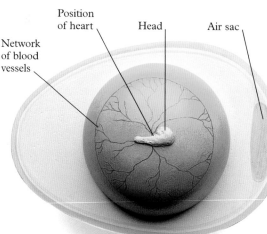

Position of heart Head Air sac

Network of blood vessels

Day three
The embryonic disc has developed into an embryo. Its heart pumps blood through a network of blood vessels. The blood collects food from the yolk and carries it to the embryo.

Wrap-around membrane
The chorion contains blood vessels that collect oxygen seeping into the egg.

Tight fit
The chick fills the whole of the egg. The yolk has been completely used up.

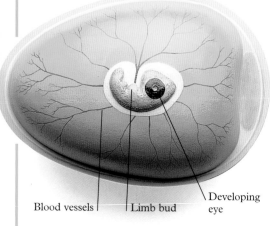

Blood vessels Limb bud Developing eye

Day seven
The embryo is now growing fast. Its eyes are developing, and it also has small limb buds that will grow into legs and wings. Oxygen from the air seeps through tiny pores in the shell, and is carried to the embryo by blood vessels.

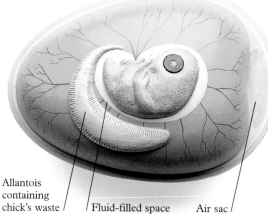

Allantois containing chick's waste Fluid-filled space Air sac

Day 12
The embryo's limb buds are now much bigger, and its head and beak are beginning to take shape. Tiny spots show where the feathers will grow and a special sac called the allantois is filling with the chick's waste.

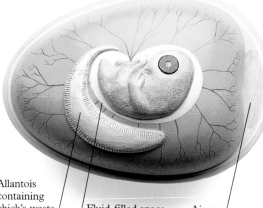

Waste sac
The allantois collects the chick's waste so that it is not poisoned inside the shell.

Day 20
The chick has just one more day to go before it hatches. It has used up all the food in the yolk, and has grown a complete covering of feathers. The chick will hatch by pecking at the egg's shell until it breaks.

How a chicken's egg develops
Like most other birds, chickens incubate their eggs, which means they sit on them to keep them warm. In chickens, incubation does not start until the last egg has been laid, but from then on, it has to continue non-stop or the chicks will die. Chicken eggs contain a large amount of yolk. This provides enough food for the embryos to turn into well-developed chicks.

Rolling around

This nesting oystercatcher is about to use her beak to rearrange her eggs. By doing this, she makes sure that all the eggs stay at an even temperature. When she moves an egg, the yolk inside turns to keep the embryo facing upwards.

Taking turns

In many birds, the female takes charge of incubating the eggs. Ostriches are different. Several females often lay in the same nest, and they sometimes sit on the nest during the day. At night, the male takes over incubation.

Eye
Unlike many young birds, a chick can see as soon as it hatches.

Ready to run
The chick's legs are fully developed, so that it will be able to run to keep up with its mother.

Easy exit
The shell's curved shape makes it easier to break from the inside than the outside.

Egg tooth
The chick uses this hard bump near the tip of its beak to help it chip its way through the shell.

Air supply
A few hours before hatching, the chick breaks into the air sac, and starts to breathe air for the first time.

Packed flat
The chick's feathers lie flat inside the egg, but when it hatches they soon dry out and fluff up.

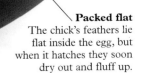

Parasite parents

Hidden away inside another animal's intestines, a tapeworm lives in a world that is full of food. It never has to move around to eat, and it never has to fight off any enemies. Instead, it can put all its energies into one extremely important task – making millions and millions of eggs. Parasites are extremely common in the animal kingdom. All of them live on or inside other animals' bodies, and all of them have to find some way to spread. Parasites like the tapeworm produce as many eggs or young as possible to increase the chances that at least a few will manage to find new hosts. Tapeworms are also passed to new hosts through infected meat.

This parasitic copepod feeds on shark's skin

Hooked head
In some tapeworms, a ring of hooks helps the worm to stay in place.

Sticky grip
Suckers cling onto the lining of the host's intestines.

Endless eggs
Tapeworms infect both animals and people. The adult worms fasten themselves in position in the host's intestines using hooks and suckers on their heads. The rest of their bodies are devoted solely to making eggs. Each section of a tapeworm's body contains a complete set of male and female organs. After the eggs have been fertilized, the sections break off and are carried out of the host animal.

Changing shape
The sections become flatter as they develop.

Growth area
The worm's body sections, or proglottids, form behind its head. More are added all the time.

Conveyor belt
As the sections get older, their sex organs start to form.

Male sex organs
The section's sperm cells develop in a network of tubes.

Sperm duct
This carries sperm cells to the section's genital pore.

Genital pore
This allows the section's sperm to escape. It also lets sperm enter from outside, so that they can fertilize the eggs.

Uterus
The uterus stores the eggs. In some tapeworms, the eggs start developing into embryos straight away.

Production line
The egg cells leave the ovary one by one. As they move towards the uterus, they are fertilized. They also get a coating of yolk.

Ovary
The ovary, which makes the eggs, consists of two branched lobes.

Yolk glands
These glands produce the yolk that is added to the eggs.

Feeding a giant
The baby cuckoo (on the left) is being fed by its "foster parent", an adult reed warbler. Cuckoos are brood parasites, which means they fool other birds into raising their young. Despite the young cuckoo's gigantic size, this reed warbler does not realize that it has been tricked.

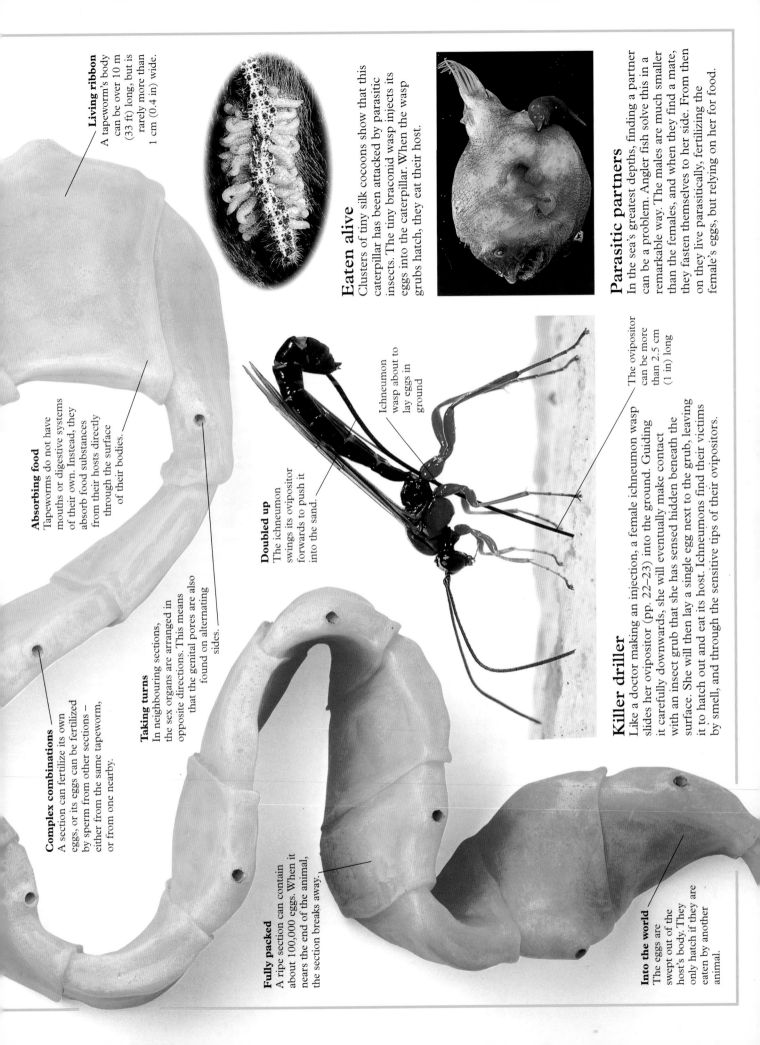

Living ribbon
A tapeworm's body can be over 10 m (33 ft) long, but is rarely more than 1 cm (0.4 in) wide.

Absorbing food
Tapeworms do not have mouths or digestive systems of their own. Instead, they absorb food substances from their hosts directly through the surface of their bodies.

Complex combinations
A section can fertilize its own eggs, or its eggs can be fertilized by sperm from other sections – either from the same tapeworm, or from one nearby.

Taking turns
In neighbouring sections, the sex organs are arranged in opposite directions. This means that the genital pores are also found on alternating sides.

Fully packed
A ripe section can contain about 100,000 eggs. When it nears the end of the animal, the section breaks away.

Eaten alive
Clusters of tiny silk cocoons show that this caterpillar has been attacked by parasitic insects. The tiny braconid wasp injects its eggs into the caterpillar. When the wasp grubs hatch, they eat their host.

Parasitic partners
In the sea's greatest depths, finding a partner can be a problem. Angler fish solve this in a remarkable way. The males are much smaller than the females, and when they find a mate, they fasten themselves to her side. From then on they live parasitically, fertilizing the female's eggs, but relying on her for food.

Doubled up
The ichneumon swings its ovipositor forwards to push it into the sand.

Ichneumon wasp about to lay eggs in ground

The ovipositor can be more than 2.5 cm (1 in) long

Killer driller
Like a doctor making an injection, a female ichneumon wasp slides her ovipositor (pp. 22–23) into the ground. Guiding it carefully downwards, she will eventually make contact with an insect grub that she has sensed hidden beneath the surface. She will then lay a single egg next to the grub, leaving it to hatch out and eat its host. Ichneumons find their victims by smell, and through the sensitive tips of their ovipositors.

Into the world
The eggs are swept out of the host's body. They only hatch if they are eaten by another animal.

Egg-laying mammals

There are 4,000 species of mammals in the world, and almost all of them give birth to live young. In Australia and New Guinea, however, there are three amazing animals known as monotremes. They have warm blood, fur, and feed their young milk like other mammals. But, instead of giving birth to live young, they lay tiny eggs. Two species of monotremes, called echidnas or spiny anteaters, are covered in sharp quills. The female has a pouch in which she incubates a single egg. The third species, the duck-billed platypus, does not have a pouch. Instead, the female incubates her eggs in a waterside burrow.

Laid back

This female echidna is lying on her back, showing her pouch. It is formed by two flaps of swollen skin that run lengthways underneath her body. After a young echidna hatches, it has to crawl towards the front of the pouch to reach its mother's milk.

Echidna egg

An echidna's egg is the size of a small grape. It has a leathery shell, and fits into a pocket at the rear end of the mother's pouch. The short-nosed echidna's egg takes about 11 days to hatch.

Newly hatched

This baby echidna is less than 15 mm (0.6 in) long. Although it is poorly developed, its stubby front legs already have tiny claws for gripping its mother's fur. After hatching, it clambers forwards for its first meal of milk.

Fur is sparser around edge of the pouch

Soft fur
The skin on an echidna's underside does not have spines. It is covered with soft fur.

Ant-proof underside
Tough skin protects the echidna from biting ants that often swarm over it as it feeds.

Muscle pouch
Instead of being bag-shaped, the echidna's pouch is formed by two ridges of muscle that run along its underside.

Mammal with a beak

As well as laying eggs, the duck-billed platypus has two other extraordinary features. Its mouth is shaped like a duck's beak, and the males have poisonous claws. It uses its beak to forage for small animals underwater, and males probably use their poison claws to fend off rivals. When the first stuffed platypus reached Europe, scientists were so suspicious of it that they decided it was a hoax.

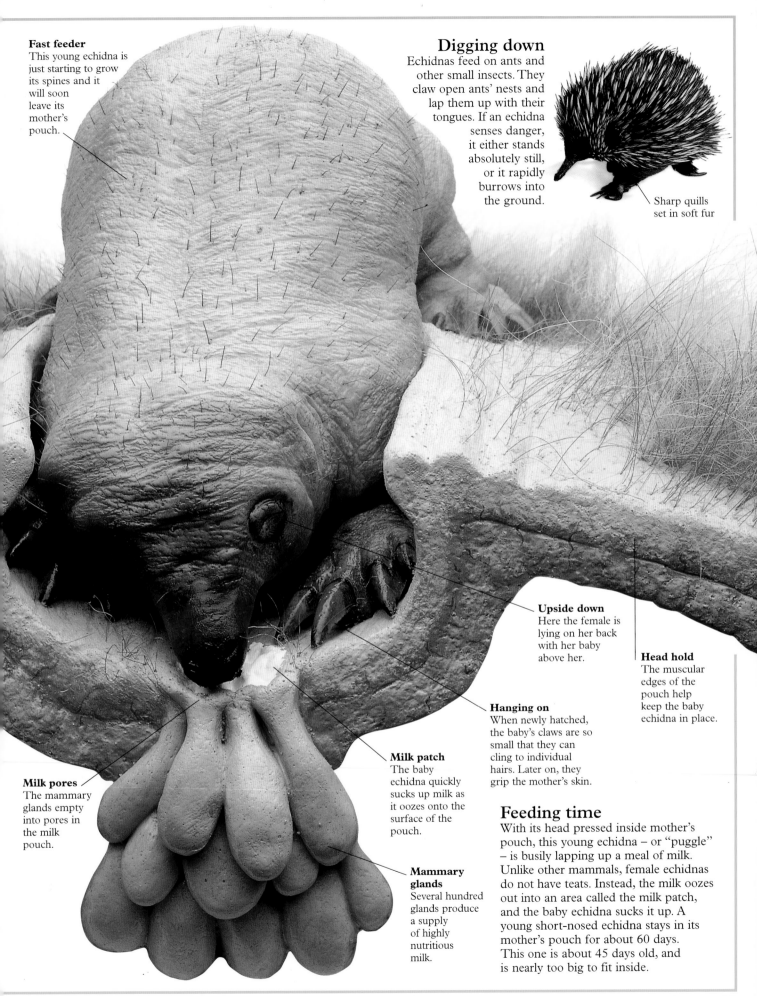

Fast feeder
This young echidna is just starting to grow its spines and it will soon leave its mother's pouch.

Digging down
Echidnas feed on ants and other small insects. They claw open ants' nests and lap them up with their tongues. If an echidna senses danger, it either stands absolutely still, or it rapidly burrows into the ground.

Sharp quills set in soft fur

Upside down
Here the female is lying on her back with her baby above her.

Head hold
The muscular edges of the pouch help keep the baby echidna in place.

Hanging on
When newly hatched, the baby's claws are so small that they can cling to individual hairs. Later on, they grip the mother's skin.

Milk patch
The baby echidna quickly sucks up milk as it oozes onto the surface of the pouch.

Milk pores
The mammary glands empty into pores in the milk pouch.

Mammary glands
Several hundred glands produce a supply of highly nutritious milk.

Feeding time
With its head pressed inside mother's pouch, this young echidna – or "puggle" – is busily lapping up a meal of milk. Unlike other mammals, female echidnas do not have teats. Instead, the milk oozes out into an area called the milk patch, and the baby echidna sucks it up. A young short-nosed echidna stays in its mother's pouch for about 60 days. This one is about 45 days old, and is nearly too big to fit inside.

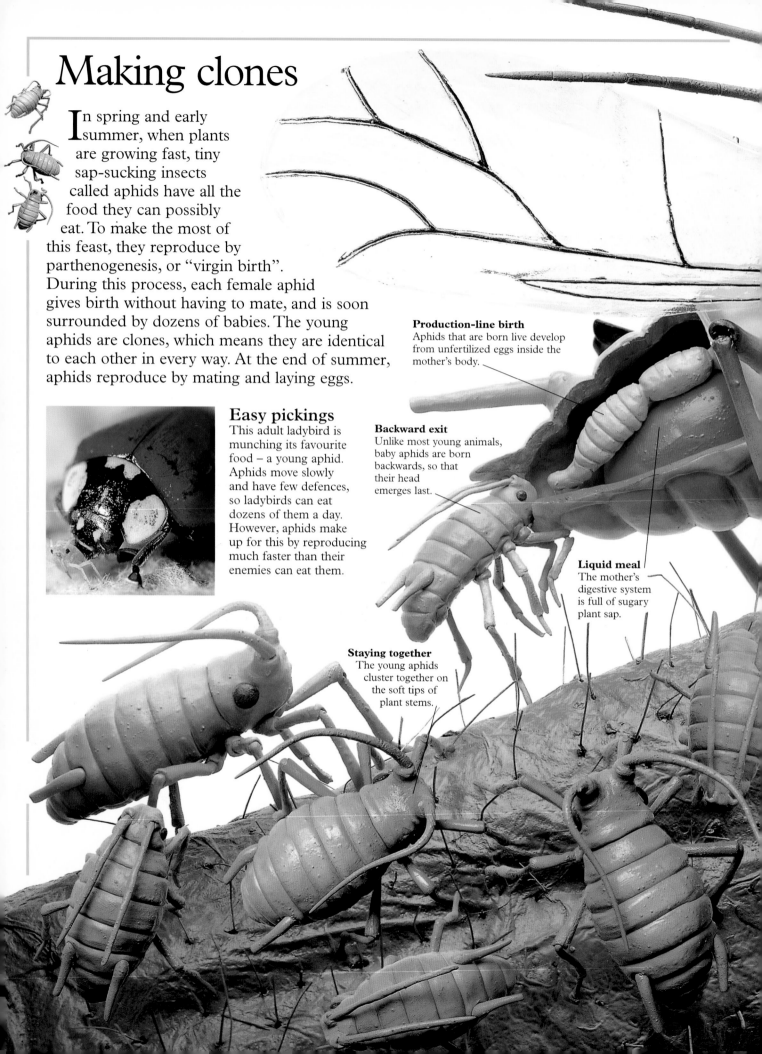

Making clones

In spring and early summer, when plants are growing fast, tiny sap-sucking insects called aphids have all the food they can possibly eat. To make the most of this feast, they reproduce by parthenogenesis, or "virgin birth". During this process, each female aphid gives birth without having to mate, and is soon surrounded by dozens of babies. The young aphids are clones, which means they are identical to each other in every way. At the end of summer, aphids reproduce by mating and laying eggs.

Easy pickings
This adult ladybird is munching its favourite food – a young aphid. Aphids move slowly and have few defences, so ladybirds can eat dozens of them a day. However, aphids make up for this by reproducing much faster than their enemies can eat them.

Production-line birth
Aphids that are born live develop from unfertilized eggs inside the mother's body.

Backward exit
Unlike most young animals, baby aphids are born backwards, so that their head emerges last.

Liquid meal
The mother's digestive system is full of sugary plant sap.

Staying together
The young aphids cluster together on the soft tips of plant stems.

Fast breeder

Every day a female aphid can give birth to as many as six young. In spring and early summer, the young are always female. Several all-female generations follow each other, but in late summer male aphids begin to appear. The females then mate with the males and lay eggs.

Cloning lizards

Several kinds of whiptail lizard from North America can reproduce by "virgin birth". However, rather than give birth to live young like aphids, whiptail lizards lay eggs. The babies are always female; males have never been found.

Piercing mouthparts

Stuck in
Aphids feed by piercing plant stems with their sharp mouthparts. These fold back when not in use.

Inside story

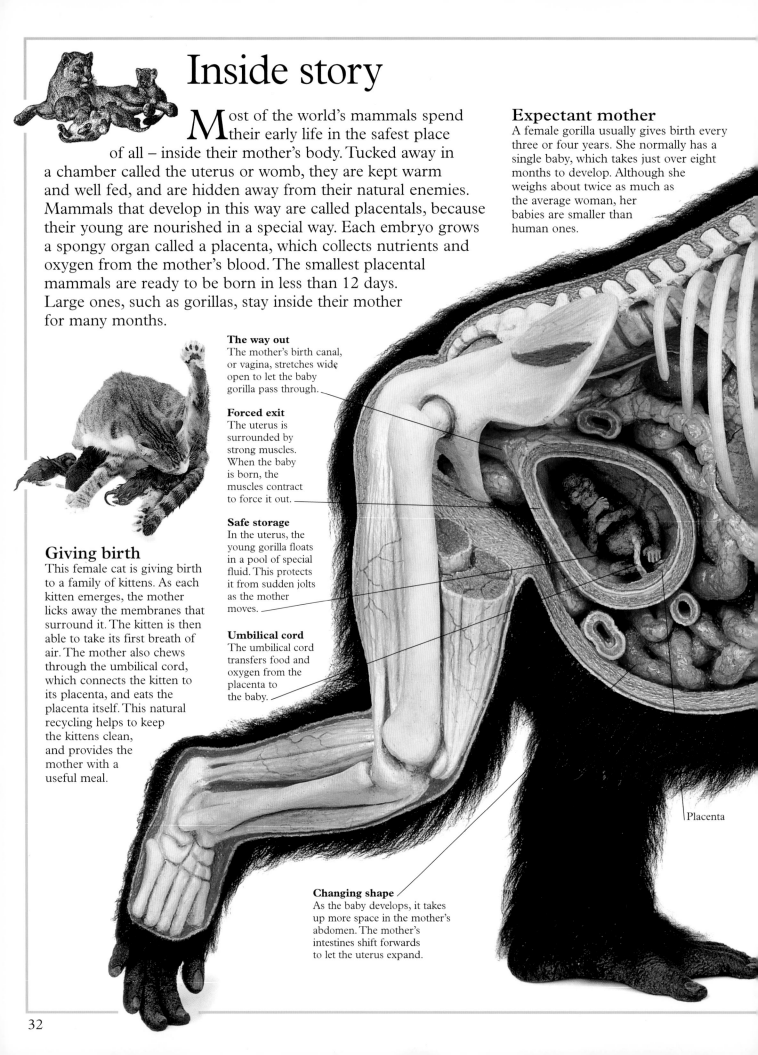

Most of the world's mammals spend their early life in the safest place of all – inside their mother's body. Tucked away in a chamber called the uterus or womb, they are kept warm and well fed, and are hidden away from their natural enemies. Mammals that develop in this way are called placentals, because their young are nourished in a special way. Each embryo grows a spongy organ called a placenta, which collects nutrients and oxygen from the mother's blood. The smallest placental mammals are ready to be born in less than 12 days. Large ones, such as gorillas, stay inside their mother for many months.

Expectant mother

A female gorilla usually gives birth every three or four years. She normally has a single baby, which takes just over eight months to develop. Although she weighs about twice as much as the average woman, her babies are smaller than human ones.

The way out
The mother's birth canal, or vagina, stretches wide open to let the baby gorilla pass through.

Forced exit
The uterus is surrounded by strong muscles. When the baby is born, the muscles contract to force it out.

Safe storage
In the uterus, the young gorilla floats in a pool of special fluid. This protects it from sudden jolts as the mother moves.

Umbilical cord
The umbilical cord transfers food and oxygen from the placenta to the baby.

Giving birth

This female cat is giving birth to a family of kittens. As each kitten emerges, the mother licks away the membranes that surround it. The kitten is then able to take its first breath of air. The mother also chews through the umbilical cord, which connects the kitten to its placenta, and eats the placenta itself. This natural recycling helps to keep the kittens clean, and provides the mother with a useful meal.

Placenta

Changing shape
As the baby develops, it takes up more space in the mother's abdomen. The mother's intestines shift forwards to let the uterus expand.

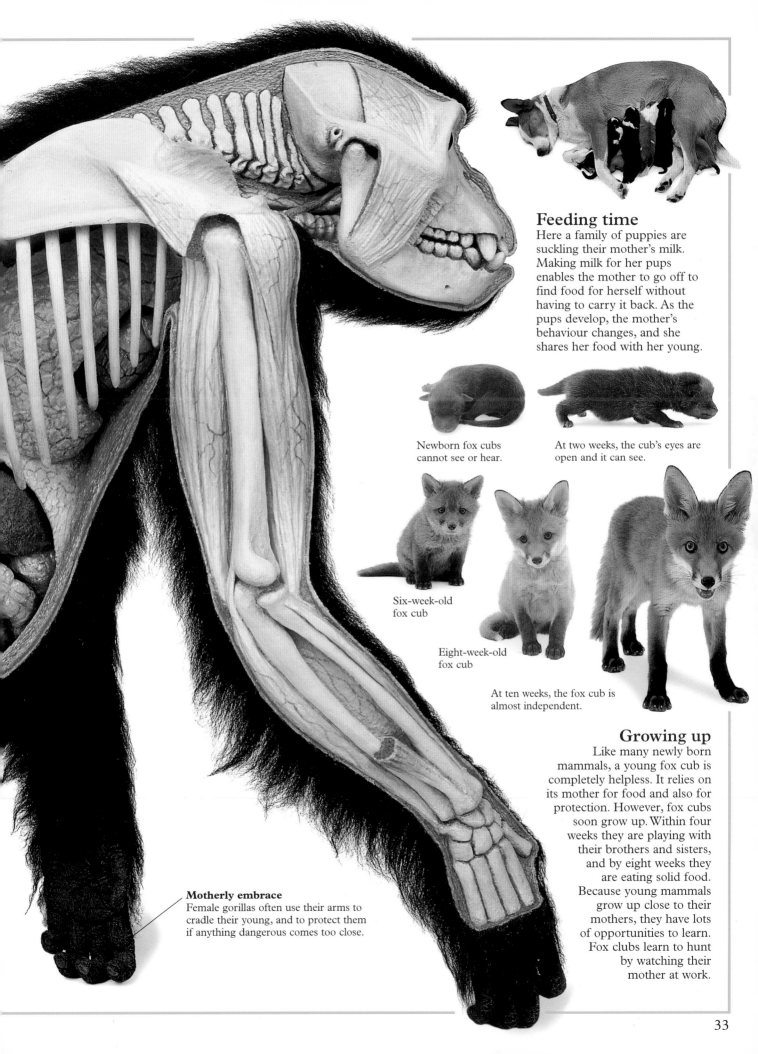

Feeding time

Here a family of puppies are suckling their mother's milk. Making milk for her pups enables the mother to go off to find food for herself without having to carry it back. As the pups develop, the mother's behaviour changes, and she shares her food with her young.

Newborn fox cubs cannot see or hear.

At two weeks, the cub's eyes are open and it can see.

Six-week-old fox cub

Eight-week-old fox cub

At ten weeks, the fox cub is almost independent.

Growing up

Like many newly born mammals, a young fox cub is completely helpless. It relies on its mother for food and also for protection. However, fox cubs soon grow up. Within four weeks they are playing with their brothers and sisters, and by eight weeks they are eating solid food. Because young mammals grow up close to their mothers, they have lots of opportunities to learn. Fox clubs learn to hunt by watching their mother at work.

Motherly embrace
Female gorillas often use their arms to cradle their young, and to protect them if anything dangerous comes too close.

Mobile homes

Marsupial frog carries tadpoles in a pouch

Many animals protect their eggs by making nests. However, a number of animals have a different way of keeping their eggs safe. After the eggs have been laid, one of the parents picks them up and carries them until they hatch. These living egg-carriers include insects, spiders, crustaceans, and frogs, but the strangest of all is the Surinam toad. In this species, as the female lays her eggs in the water, the male fastens them in place on her back. Once the eggs are in position, a special layer of spongy skin grows up around them, and completely hides them while they develop. After many weeks the young break out of their mobile home. Instead of emerging as tadpoles, like most young amphibians, they are released as tiny toads.

On-board development
After each egg hatches, a tadpole develops inside the chamber.

Getting oxygen
During their development, the tadpoles absorb oxygen through their skins and tails.

Break-out
The young emerge by pushing open the lid on their chambers. Any part of their body can come first.

Locked inside
A tough lid covers each egg and protects it as it develops.

Separate quarters
Each egg becomes surrounded by skin, forming a chamber on the toad's back.

Fully formed
The newly-emerged toads are like miniature versions of their parents.

Spongy skin
The spongy layer develops within hours of mating and egg-laying. It remains until the baby toads have emerged.

Temporarily grounded
In some giant water bugs, the female cements the eggs onto her partner's wings, and he carries them until they hatch. Water bugs are strong fliers, but a male with eggs cannot use his wings.

Surinam toad
This bizarre-looking amphibian lives in murky streams in tropical South America. Just before the female is ready to lay her eggs, the male grips her by the waist. The pair then carry out a series of underwater somersaults, with the female laying eggs while she is upside down. Using his back legs and body, the male presses the eggs onto the female's back, and they later become embedded in her swollen skin.

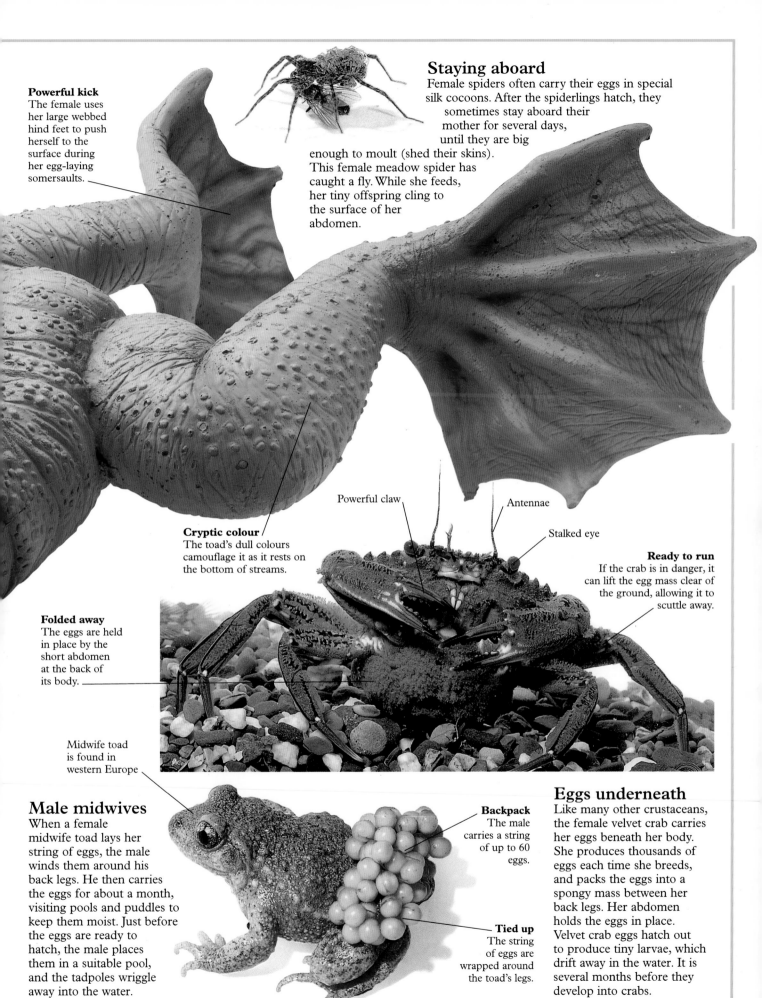

Powerful kick
The female uses her large webbed hind feet to push herself to the surface during her egg-laying somersaults.

Staying aboard
Female spiders often carry their eggs in special silk cocoons. After the spiderlings hatch, they sometimes stay aboard their mother for several days, until they are big enough to moult (shed their skins). This female meadow spider has caught a fly. While she feeds, her tiny offspring cling to the surface of her abdomen.

Cryptic colour
The toad's dull colours camouflage it as it rests on the bottom of streams.

Powerful claw

Antennae

Stalked eye

Ready to run
If the crab is in danger, it can lift the egg mass clear of the ground, allowing it to scuttle away.

Folded away
The eggs are held in place by the short abdomen at the back of its body.

Midwife toad is found in western Europe

Male midwives
When a female midwife toad lays her string of eggs, the male winds them around his back legs. He then carries the eggs for about a month, visiting pools and puddles to keep them moist. Just before the eggs are ready to hatch, the male places them in a suitable pool, and the tadpoles wriggle away into the water.

Backpack
The male carries a string of up to 60 eggs.

Tied up
The string of eggs are wrapped around the toad's legs.

Eggs underneath
Like many other crustaceans, the female velvet crab carries her eggs beneath her body. She produces thousands of eggs each time she breeds, and packs the eggs into a spongy mass between her back legs. Her abdomen holds the eggs in place. Velvet crab eggs hatch out to produce tiny larvae, which drift away in the water. It is several months before they develop into crabs.

Caring parents

For the first days or weeks of life, baby animals are often in danger. They are small and inexperienced, which makes them easy prey. However, their chances of survival are greatly increased if they are looked after by their parents. Parent animals care for their young in many different ways. Some of them stand guard over their young, and attack anything that comes too close. Many build special nests or dens, where their young are hidden from predators and protected from the weather outside. Some extraordinary fish go further than this. They use their bodies as living shelters, and let their young swim aboard when danger threatens.

Fatherly care
Female seahorses place their newly laid eggs into a special pouch on the front of the male's body. The male incubates the young, and protects them when they are newly hatched. When the young are ready to leave the pouch, the male looks as if he is giving birth.

Tail clings to underwater plants

Pregnant pouch
The male's pouch swells up during the breeding season. It has a small opening that receives the eggs.

Going out
When the coast is clear, the mother fish closes her gill covers, pumping the young out of her mouth.

Safely stowed
The mother's mouth provides enough room for dozens of young.

Shoal of young fish

Night shelter
As they get older, the young fish spend more time outside. For the first month, they still return to their mother's mouth at night.

Time to eat
For the first few days, the young fish live on yolk from their eggs. After this they have to leave their mother's mouth to feed.

Hitching a lift
Cygnets (young swans) often clamber aboard their parents' backs when danger threatens, or when they need to rest. Cygnets usually clamber down if their parents reach underwater to feed, but other young water birds, such as grebes, cling to their parents when they dive.

Mobile mouthful
The yellow-banded cichlid is one of many mouthbrooding fish that live in African lakes and rivers. After the fish has laid her eggs, she scoops them up in her mouth. The eggs hatch, and the young fish stay in their mother's mouth until they are big enough to venture outside.

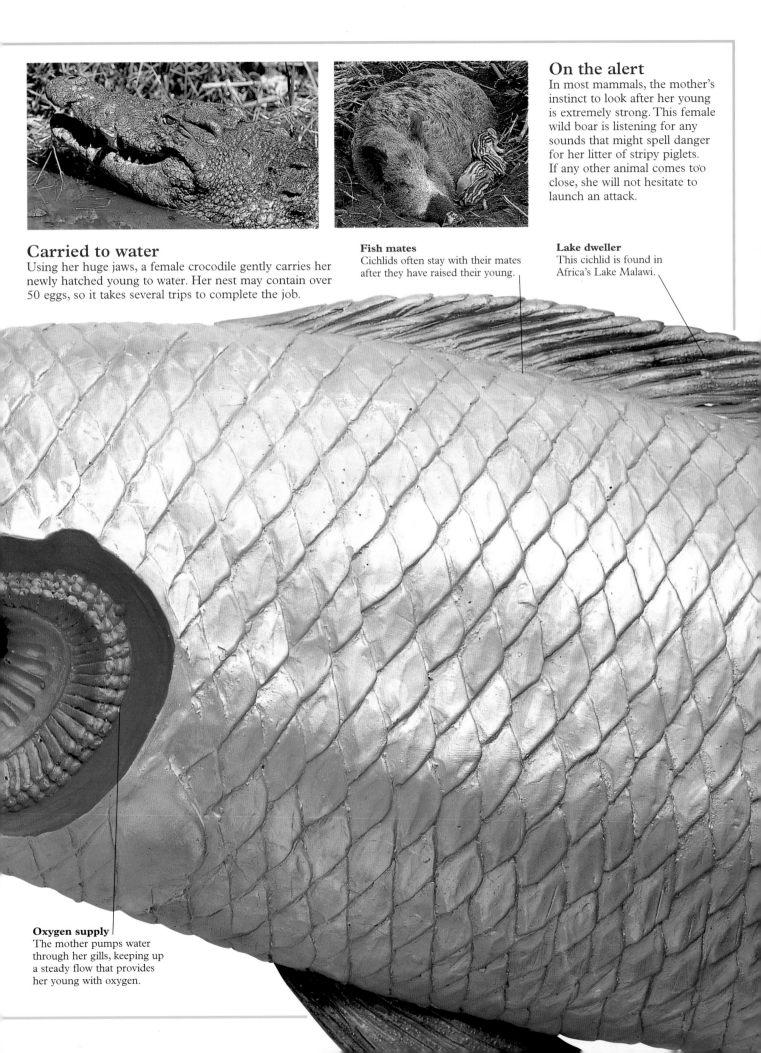

On the alert

In most mammals, the mother's instinct to look after her young is extremely strong. This female wild boar is listening for any sounds that might spell danger for her litter of stripy piglets. If any other animal comes too close, she will not hesitate to launch an attack.

Carried to water

Using her huge jaws, a female crocodile gently carries her newly hatched young to water. Her nest may contain over 50 eggs, so it takes several trips to complete the job.

Fish mates
Cichlids often stay with their mates after they have raised their young.

Lake dweller
This cichlid is found in Africa's Lake Malawi.

Oxygen supply
The mother pumps water through her gills, keeping up a steady flow that provides her young with oxygen.

Life in a pouch

Virginia opossum

When the first European settlers reached Australia, they were amazed by the animals they found there. Instead of keeping their embryos inside their bodies like most mammals do (pp. 32–33), Australia's native mammals give birth to tiny young, and then raise them in a pouch. Mammals like this are called marsupials. A marsupial's pouch is usually shaped like a bag, and is on the underside of its body. As well as protecting the young, it houses nipples from which they can feed. Marsupials are much less common than placental mammals, but they are still very well adapted for survival. A female wallaby or kangaroo can have both a newly born and a well-grown baby, or joey, feeding from her pouch at the same time. This allows her to nurture two generations of young at once.

1 To prepare for the birth, the mother licks a clear path through her fur for the joey to follow.

2 Joeys are born at a very early stage of their development. This joey is about 2 cm (0.75 in) long, and weighs less than 5 g (0.2 oz). Only its front legs work, and it uses these to haul itself forward on the marathon journey from the birth canal to the pouch's opening.

3 Once in the pouch, the joey fastens its mouth to one of its mother's nipples. For the next four months, it will not leave the pouch, and grows all the time.

Feeding station
The nipple grows in step with the joey, and eventually becomes about 10 cm (4 in) long.

Ready for use
A newly born joey fastens itself to one of the smallest nipples.

Plenty to spare
A kangaroo's pouch usually contains four nipples.

Stepping out
After developing in the pouch, a young kangaroo or wallaby begins to try out life outside. It still reaches into the pouch to drink milk, and climbs back inside if danger threatens. Meanwhile, a new joey has reached the pouch and begun to grow.

Adult wallaby

This way round
Kangaroos and wallabies have forward-facing pouches.

Young wallaby

Embryos in reserve
Embryos are stored until they are needed. A new embryo starts to develop when a joey is about to leave the pouch.

Return trip
The joey suckles milk for up to a year after leaving the pouch.

Tight grip
A young koala spends six months in its mother's pouch, and then climbs out and clings onto her back. The koala's pouch has a narrow entrance to stop the young falling out.

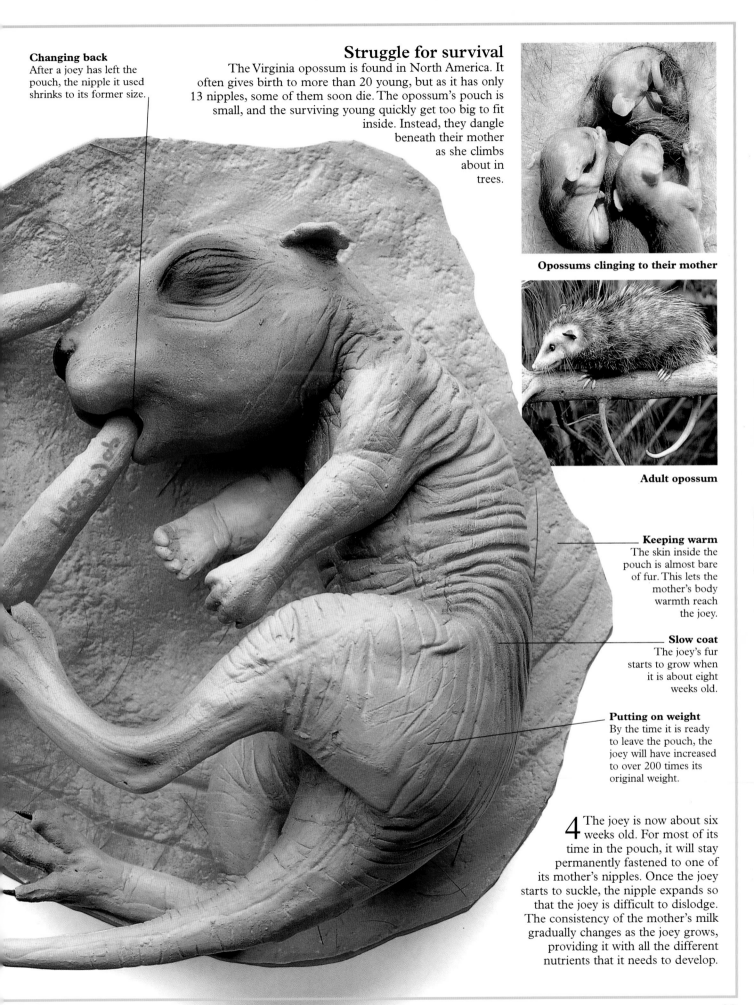

Changing back
After a joey has left the pouch, the nipple it used shrinks to its former size.

Struggle for survival
The Virginia opossum is found in North America. It often gives birth to more than 20 young, but as it has only 13 nipples, some of them soon die. The opossum's pouch is small, and the surviving young quickly get too big to fit inside. Instead, they dangle beneath their mother as she climbs about in trees.

Opossums clinging to their mother

Adult opossum

Keeping warm
The skin inside the pouch is almost bare of fur. This lets the mother's body warmth reach the joey.

Slow coat
The joey's fur starts to grow when it is about eight weeks old.

Putting on weight
By the time it is ready to leave the pouch, the joey will have increased to over 200 times its original weight.

4 The joey is now about six weeks old. For most of its time in the pouch, it will stay permanently fastened to one of its mother's nipples. Once the joey starts to suckle, the nipple expands so that the joey is difficult to dislodge. The consistency of the mother's milk gradually changes as the joey grows, providing it with all the different nutrients that it needs to develop.

39

Changing shape

Tadpole – the larva of a frog

All animals change as they grow up. In some animals the young start life looking similar to their parents, but in others the changes are far-reaching, and the animal's body is entirely transformed. This drastic change of shape is called metamorphosis. It allows the adult and the young to live in totally different ways from each other. They can perform different roles, eat different types of food, and inhabit different environments. Apart from fish and amphibians, few vertebrates undergo metamorphosis. However, it is very common in less complex creatures – particularly in animals that spend their lives in water.

Live-in larva

A larva is any young animal that changes shape completely as it grows up. This is the larva of a caddisfly, an insect that spends the first part of its life in water. Caddisfly larvae protect themselves from being eaten by other water animals by constructing tubular cases out of sand grains, tiny sticks, shells, and blades of grass.

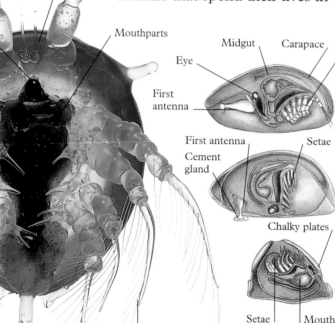

First antenna

Central naupliar eye

Frontal horn

Carapace (hard shield)

Mouthparts

Midgut

Carapace

Setae

Eye

First antenna

First antenna

Cement gland

Setae

Chalky plates

Setae

Mouth

Fringed setae (legs)

Tail

1 After weeks adrift at sea, the nauplius larva of a barnacle changes into a cyprid larva. Unlike the nauplius larva, the cyprid larva does not feed.

2 If the cyprid larva settles on a suitable rock, it begins to change into an adult. First, it cements itself in position.

3 The larva becomes enclosed by chalky plates. Its "feet" now point upwards, so they can be used to collect food.

Life adrift
Unless you are a marine biologist, you might have trouble identifying this strange-looking animal. Amazingly, it is the "nauplius" larva of a barnacle – an animal that spends its adult life fastened in one place. In contrast, barnacle larvae drift about in the sea.

Settling down
Like barnacles, crabs spend the first part of their lives as larvae that drift in the sea. A young crab larva, called a zoea, has long spines and feathery legs. It changes into a megalopa larva which settles on the sea floor. This in turn becomes a miniature adult crab.

Megalopa larva

Shaped for strength
The barnacle's plates fit together to form a conical shape – ideal for withstanding the battering of the waves.

Adult box crab

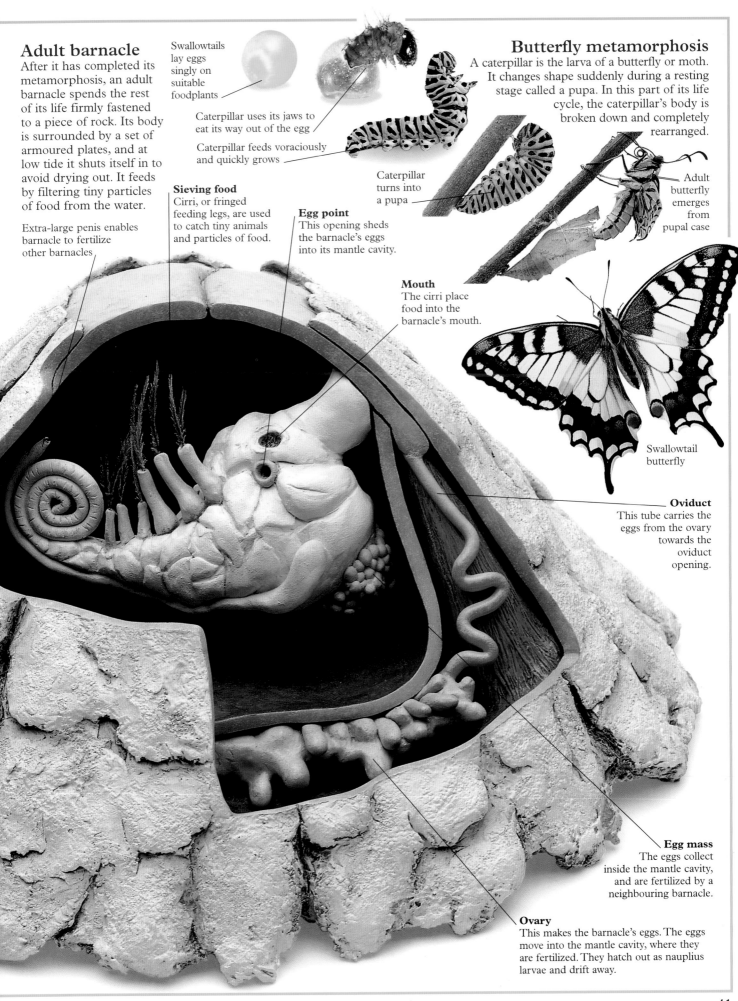

Adult barnacle

After it has completed its metamorphosis, an adult barnacle spends the rest of its life firmly fastened to a piece of rock. Its body is surrounded by a set of armoured plates, and at low tide it shuts itself in to avoid drying out. It feeds by filtering tiny particles of food from the water.

Extra-large penis enables barnacle to fertilize other barnacles

Swallowtails lay eggs singly on suitable foodplants

Caterpillar uses its jaws to eat its way out of the egg

Caterpillar feeds voraciously and quickly grows

Sieving food
Cirri, or fringed feeding legs, are used to catch tiny animals and particles of food.

Egg point
This opening sheds the barnacle's eggs into its mantle cavity.

Caterpillar turns into a pupa

Mouth
The cirri place food into the barnacle's mouth.

Butterfly metamorphosis

A caterpillar is the larva of a butterfly or moth. It changes shape suddenly during a resting stage called a pupa. In this part of its life cycle, the caterpillar's body is broken down and completely rearranged.

Adult butterfly emerges from pupal case

Swallowtail butterfly

Oviduct
This tube carries the eggs from the ovary towards the oviduct opening.

Egg mass
The eggs collect inside the mantle cavity, and are fertilized by a neighbouring barnacle.

Ovary
This makes the barnacle's eggs. The eggs move into the mantle cavity, where they are fertilized. They hatch out as nauplius larvae and drift away.

Glossary

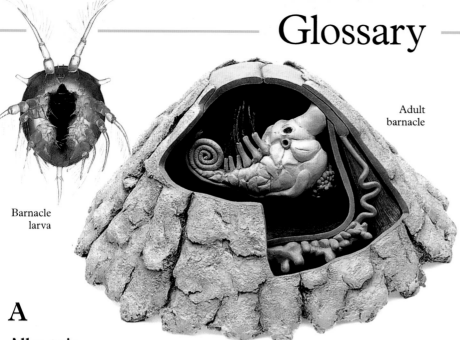

Barnacle larva

Adult barnacle

A

Allantois
A special bag-like membrane attached to an embryo. It collects waste and sometimes helps to gather oxygen.

Asexual reproduction
Any kind of reproduction that involves only a single parent.

B

Breeding season
The part of an animal's life when it is able to breed. Many animals have just one breeding season a year.

Budding
A kind of reproduction in which young animals grow from buds on their parents.

C

Chorion
The outer covering of an embryo.

Clone
A collection of identical living things that come from the same parent and share exactly the same genes.

Courtship
A special kind of behaviour used by animals to attract a mate.

E

Egg cell
A special female cell that can produce a new animal. To develop, egg cells (ova) usually have to be fertilized by sperms.

Embryo
A young animal in the early stages of development.

Embryonic disc
The patch of cells in a bird's egg that develops into a young bird.

Eusocial species
A species that lives in large family groups, known as colonies. In each colony, only one female reproduces. She is known as the queen.

F

Fertilization
The joining together of a male and a female cell (sperm and egg) to produce a new living thing.

Follicle
A small cluster of cells that surrounds an egg cell. Follicles are found in female organs called ovaries.

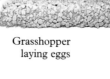

Grasshopper laying eggs

G

Genes
The chemical instructions that make living things work.

H

Hatching
Breaking out of an egg. Some animals hatch by eating their way out, but other animals have to break or tear open the shell of the egg.

Hermaphrodite
Any animal (or plant) that has both male and female reproductive organs.

I

Incubate
To sit on eggs. Incubation keeps eggs warm, and enables them to develop.

Internal fertilization
Fertilization that takes place inside the mother's body.

L

Larva
A young animal that develops by changing shape.

M

Mammary gland
A gland in female mammals that produces milk.

Marsupial
A mammal that raises its young in a pouch. The young are born while their development is still at an early stage.

Metamorphosis
A complete change in body shape that takes place as some animals develop.

Milk
A liquid food made by female mammals for their young.

Monotreme
A mammal that reproduces by laying eggs. Monotremes are only found in Australia and New Guinea.

N

Nest
Any kind of shelter made by animals to protect themselves or their eggs and young from predators and the weather.

Nipple
The place where young mammals suckle milk from their mother. Also known as a teat.

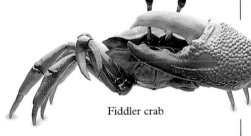
Fiddler crab

O

Ovary
In female animals, the reproductive organ that makes egg cells, or ova.

Oviduct
A tube that carries ova out of a female animal's ovaries.

Oviparous
A word used for any animal that reproduces by laying eggs.

Ovo-viviparous
Animals that lay their eggs at the moment that they are ready to hatch.

Ovipositor
A tube-like organ that some female animals use when laying eggs.

P

Parthenogenesis
Reproduction using egg cells that do not need to be fertilized.

Penis
The external organ used by male animals to introduce sperm cells into the female's body.

Pouch
In marsupials, a special chamber on the outside of the mother's body that is used to house the developing young.

Placenta
A spongy pad attached to an embryo animal that collects food and oxygen from its mother.

Pregnancy
The period of time that a female animal carries her unborn young inside her body.

S

Sexual reproduction
Reproduction that involves a male and a female parent, or more rarely, parents that are both sexes at once.

Spermatophore
A package containing sperm cells.

Sperm cell
A special kind of male cell that fertilizes egg cells to create a new animal.

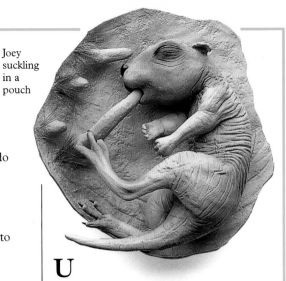
Joey suckling in a pouch

U

Umbilical cord
A cord that connects an embryo to a placenta. It carries food to the embryo from its mother, and carries away waste.

Uterus
The organ inside female mammals that protects developing young.

V

Vagina
The channel that connects a female mammal's uterus to the outside.

Viviparous
A word used to describe animals that give birth to live young.

Y

Yolk
The nutritious substance inside an egg that supplies a developing animal with food.

Burmese python laying egg

Index

Acknowledgements

The publisher would like to thank: Phil Manning, University of Sheffield, and Mark O'Shea for advice. Maggie Tingle for design assistance. Jayne Parsons and Miranda Smith for proof-reading. Marion Dent for the index. Special thanks to Robert Graham for his excellent research.

Artwork: Dominic Zwemmer

Jacket design: Sophia Tampakopoulos

Additional photography: Jane Burton, Steve Gorton, Frank Greenaway, Kim Taylor, Harry Taylor, Mike Linley, and Dave King.

Picture Credits:
Key: t=top; b=below; c= centre; l=left; r=right

Kiyokazu Agata @ Himeji Institute of Technology 11bc;
Aquila Photographic: Les Baker 26cl;
Ardea London Ltd: John Clegg 10cl; Pascal Goetgheluck 17cl; Valerie Taylor 24tr;
Bruce Coleman: Fred Bruemmer 23tr; Dr.Eckart Pott 14bl; Andrew J.Purcell 14cl; Kevin Rushby 25bl; Kim Taylor 19tr;
Frank Lane Picture Agency: K. Maslowski 3tr; P Perry 36bc; Roger Tidman 12clb; Chris Mattison: 20cl; 31tr;
Nature Focus: Rismac 28cl, clb, tr;
Natural History Photographic Agency: A.N.T. 2br; Ashod Francis Papazian 40bc; Peter Parks 40cb; John Shaw 3cr; Norbert Wu 27br;
Oxford Scientific Films: Animals, Animals/ Ralph Reinhold 12tr; G.I. Bernard 11cb; Scott Camazine/M.

Marchetorre 11tr; Wolfgang Lummer/Okapia 37tr; Harold Taylor/Abipp 30cl; Konrad Wothe 17cl; David Parker/Elizabeth Parker-Cook: 28bl;
Planet Earth Pictures: Geoff du Feu 15tl; Roger de la Harpe 37tl; Stephen P. Hopkin 8clb, 10br; 14tr W.B.Irwin 25br; Ken Lucas 34bl;
Premaphotos Wildlife: K.G. Preston-Mafham 24tr, 27cr;
Science Photo Library: J.C. Revy 22tr;
Warren Photographic: Jane Burton 15tc; Kim Taylor 35tc.